PR 6023.E25 LED

ISBN: 9781290917377

Published by:
HardPress Publishing
8345 NW 66TH ST #2561
MIAMI FL 33166-2626

Email: info@hardpress.net
Web: http://www.hardpress.net

LAST
SONGS

BY THE SAME AUTHOR

SONGS OF THE FIELDS
THIRD EDITION

SONGS OF PEACE

LAST SONGS

BY
FRANCIS
LEDWIDGE

HERBERT   JENKINS   LIMITED
YORK STREET, ST. JAMES'S
LONDON, S.W. 1 ❦ MCMXVIII

WILLIAM BRENDON AND SON, LTD., PRINTERS, PLYMOUTH, ENGLAND

INTRODUCTION

WRITING amidst rather too much noise and squalor to do justice at all to the delicate rustic muse of Francis Ledwidge, I do not like to delay his book any longer, nor to fail in a promise long ago made to him to write this introduction. He has gone down in that vast maelstrom into which poets do well to adventure and from which their country might perhaps be wise to withhold them, but that is our Country's affair. He has left behind him verses of great beauty, simple rural lyrics that may be something of an anodyne for this stricken age. If ever an age needed beautiful little songs our age needs them; and I know few songs

more peaceful and happy, or better suited
to soothe the scars on the mind of those
who have looked on certain places, of which
the prophecy in the gospels seems no more
than an ominous hint when it speaks of
the abomination of desolation.

He told me once that it was on one
particular occasion, when walking at evening through the village of Slane in summer,
that he heard a blackbird sing. The notes,
he said, were very beautiful, and it is this
blackbird that he tells of in three wonderful
lines in his early poem called " Behind the
Closed Eye," and it is this song perhaps
more than anything else that has been the
inspiration of his brief life. Dynasties
shook and the earth shook; and the war,
not yet described by any man, revelled and
and wallowed in destruction around him;
and Francis Ledwidge stayed true to his

inspiration, as his homeward songs will show.

I had hoped he would have seen the fame he has well deserved ; but it is hard for a poet to live to see fame even in times of peace. In these days it is harder than ever.

DUNSANY.

October 9th, 1917.

CONTENTS

LAST
SONGS

TO AN OLD QUILL OF LORD DUNSANY'S

BEFORE you leave my hands' abuses
To lie where many odd things meet you,
Neglected darkling of the Muses,
I, the last of singers, greet you.

Snug in some white wing they found you,
On the Common bleak and muddy,
Noisy goslings gobbling round you
In the pools of sunset, ruddy.

Have you sighed in wings untravelled
For the heights where others view the

Bluer widths of heaven, and marvelled

At the utmost top of Beauty ?

No ! it cannot be ; the soul you

Sigh with craves nor begs of us.

From such heights a poet stole you

From a wing of Pegasus.

You have been where gods were sleeping

In the dawn of new creations,

Ere they woke to woman's weeping

At the broken thrones of nations.

You have seen this old world shattered

By old gods it disappointed,

Lying up in darkness, battered

By wild comets, unanointed.

But for Beauty unmolested

Have you still the sighing olden ?

I know mountains heather-crested,

Waters white, and waters golden.

There I'd keep you, in the lowly

Beauty-haunts of bird and poet,

Sailing in a wing, the holy

Silences of lakes below it.

But I leave you by where no man

Finds you, when I too be gone

From the puddles on this common

Over the dark Rubicon.

Londonderry,
    September 18th, 1916.

B

TO A SPARROW

BECAUSE you have no fear to mingle
Wings with those of greater part,
So like me, with song I single
Your sweet impudence of heart.

And when prouder feathers go where
Summer holds her leafy show,
You still come to us from nowhere
Like grey leaves across the snow.

In back ways where odd and end go
To your meals you drop down sure,

Knowing every broken window

Of the hospitable poor.

There is no bird half so harmless,

None so sweetly rude as you,

None so common and so charmless,

None of virtues nude as you.

But for all your faults I love you,

For you linger with us still,

Though the wintry winds reprove you

And the snow is on the hill.

Londonderry,
September 20*th*, 1916.

OLD CLO'

I WAS just coming in from the garden,

Or about to go fishing for eels,

And, smiling, I asked you to pardon

My boots very low at the heels.

And I thought that you never would go,

As you stood in the doorway ajar,

For my heart would keep saying, " Old Clo',

You're found out at last as you are."

I was almost ashamed to acknowledge

That I was the quarry you sought,

For was I not bred in a college

And reared in a mansion, you thought.

And now in the latest style cut

With fortune more kinder I go

To welcome you half-ways. Ah ! but

I was nearer the gods when " Old Clo'."

YOUTH

SHE paved the way with perfume sweet
Of flowers that moved like winds alight,
And never weary grew my feet
Wandering through the spring's delight.

She dropped her sweet fife to her lips
And lured me with her melodies,
To where the great big wandering ships
Put out into the peaceful seas.

But when the year grew chill and brown,

And all the wings of Summer flown,

Within the tumult of a town

She left me to grow old alone.

THE LITTLE CHILDREN

Hunger points a bony finger
To the workhouse on the hill,
But the little children linger
While there's flowers to gather still
For my sunny window sill.

In my hands I take their faces,
Smiling to my smiles they run.
Would that I could take their places
Where the murky bye-ways shun
The benedictions of the sun

How they laugh and sing returning
Lightly on their secret way.
While I listen in my yearning
Their laughter fills the windy day
With gladness, youth and May.

AUTUMN

Now leafy winds are blowing cold,
And South by West the sun goes down,
A quiet huddles up the fold
In sheltered corners of the brown.

Like scattered fire the wild fruit strews
The ground beneath the blowing tree,
And there the busy squirrel hews
His deep and secret granary.

And when the night comes starry clear,
The lonely quail complains beside
The glistening waters on the mere
Where widowed Beauties yet abide.

26

And I, too, make my own complaint

Upon a reed I plucked in June,

And love to hear it echoed faint

Upon another heart in tune.

Londonderry,
  September 29th, 1916.

IRELAND

I CALLED you by sweet names by wood and
  linn,
You answered not because my voice was
  new,
And you were listening for the hounds of
  Finn
    And the long hosts of Lugh.

And so, I came unto a windy height
And cried my sorrow, but you heard no wind,
For you were listening to small ships in
  flight,
    And the wail on hills behind.

And then I left you, wandering the war

Arméd with will, from distant goal to goal,

To find you at the last free as of yore,

    Or die to save your soul.

And then you called to us from far and

    near

To bring your crown from out the deeps of

    time,

It is my grief your voice I couldn't hear

    In such a distant clime.

LADY FAIR

LADY fair, have we not met

In our lives elsewhere ?

Darkling in my mind to-night

Faint fair faces dare

Memory's old unfaithfulness

To what was true and fair.

Long of memory is Regret,

But what Regret has taken flight

Through my memory's silences ?

Lo ! I turn it to the light.

'Twas but a pleasure in distress,

Too faint and far off for redress.

But some light glancing in your hair

And in the liquid of your eyes

Seem to murmur old good-byes

In our lives elsewhere.

Have we not met, Lady fair ?

Londonderry,
    October 27th, 1916.

AT A POET'S GRAVE

WHEN I leave down this pipe my friend
And sleep with flowers I loved, apart,
My songs shall rise in wilding things
Whose roots are in my heart.

And here where that sweet poet sleeps
I hear the songs he left unsung,
When winds are fluttering the flowers
And summer-bells are rung.

November, 1916.

AFTER COURT MARTIAL

My mind is not my mind, therefore

I take no heed of what men say,

I lived ten thousand years before

God cursed the town of Nineveh.

The Present is a dream I see

Of horror and loud sufferings,

At dawn a bird will waken me

Unto my place among the kings.

And though men called me a vile name,

And all my dream companions gone,

'Tis I the soldier bears the shame,

Not I the king of Babylon.

A MOTHER'S SONG

LITTLE ships of whitest pearl
With sailors who were ancient kings,
Come over the sea when my little girl
Sings.

And if my little girl should weep,
Little ships with torn sails
Go headlong down among the deep
Whales.

November, 1916.

AT CURRABWEE

EVERY night at Currabwee

Little men with leather hats

Mend the boots of Faery

From the tough wings of the bats.

So my mother told to me,

And she is wise you will agree.

Louder than a cricket's wing

All night long their hammer's glee

Times the merry songs they sing

Of Ireland glorious and free.

So I heard Joseph Plunkett say,

You know he heard them but last May

And when the night is very cold

They warm their hands against the light

Of stars that make the waters gold

Where they are labouring all the night.

So Pearse said, and he knew the truth,

Among the stars he spent his youth.

And I, myself, have often heard

Their singing as the stars went by,

For am I not of those who reared

The banner of old Ireland high,

From Dublin town to Turkey's shores,

And where the Vardar loudly roars ?

December, 1916.

TWO SONGS

I WILL come no more awhile,
  Song-time is over.
A fire is burning in my heart,
  I was ever a rover.

You will hear me no more awhile,
  The birds are dumb,
And a voice in the distance calls
  " Come," and " Come."

December 13th, 1916.

UNA BAWN

UNA BAWN, the days are long,
And the seas I cross are wide,
I must go when Ireland needs,
And you must bide.

And should I not return to you
When the sails are on the tide,
'Tis you will find the days so long,
Una Bawn, and I must bide.

December 13*th*, 1916.

SPRING LOVE

I saw her coming through the flowery grass,

Round her swift ankles butterfly and bee

Blent loud and silent wings ; I saw her pass

Where foam-bows shivered on the sunny

> sea.

Then came the swallow crowding up the

> dawn,

And cuckoo-echoes filled the dewy South.

I left my love upon the hill, alone,

My last kiss burning on her lovely mouth.

B.E.F.—*December 26th*, 1916.

SOLILOQUY

WHEN I was young I had a care
Lest I should cheat me of my share
Of that which makes it sweet to strive
For life, and dying still survive,
A name in sunshine written higher
Than lark or poet dare aspire.

But I grew weary doing well,
Besides, 'twas sweeter in that hell,
Down with the loud banditti people
Who robbed the orchards, climbed the
    steeple
For jackdaws' eggs and made the cock
Crow ere 'twas daylight on the clock.

I was so very bad the neighbours
Spoke of me at their daily labours.

And now I'm drinking wine in France,
The helpless child of circumstance.
To-morrow will be loud with war,
How will I be accounted for ?

It is too late now to retrieve
A fallen dream, too late to grieve
A name unmade, but not too late
To thank the gods for what is great ;
A keen-edged sword, a soldier's heart,
Is greater than a poet's art.
And greater than a poet's fame
A little grave that has no name.

DAWN

Quiet miles of golden sky,
And in my heart a sudden flower.
I want to clap my hands and cry
For Beauty in her secret bower.

Quiet golden miles of dawn—
Smiling all the East along ;
And in my heart nigh fully blown,
A little rose-bud of a song.

CEOL SIDHE[1]

WHEN May is here, and every morn
Is dappled with pied bells,
And dewdrops glance along the thorn
And wings flash in the dells,
I take my pipe and play a tune
Of dreams, a whispered melody,
For feet that dance beneath the moon
In fairy jollity.

And when the pastoral hills are grey
And the dim stars are spread,
A scamper fills the grass like play
Of feet where fairies tread.

And many a little whispering thing

Is calling to the Shee.

The dewy bells of evening ring,

And all is melody.

[1] Fairy music

France,
December 29th, 1916.

THE RUSHES

THE rushes nod by the river

As the winds on the loud waves go,

And the things they nod of are many,

For it's many the secret they know.

And I think they are wise as the fairies

Who lived ere the hills were high,

They nod so grave by the river

To everyone passing by.

If they would tell me their secrets

I would go by a hidden way,

To the rath when the moon retiring

Dips dim horns into the gray.

46

And a fairy-girl out of Leinster

In a long dance I should meet,

My heart to her heart beating,

My feet in rhyme with her feet.

France,
   January 6th, 1917.

THE DEAD KINGS

ALL the dead kings came to me

At Rosnaree, where I was dreaming.

A few stars glimmered through the morn,

And down the thorn the dews were streaming.

And every dead king had a story

Of ancient glory, sweetly told.

It was too early for the lark,

But the starry dark had tints of gold.

I listened to the sorrows three

Of that Eirë passed into song.

A cock crowed near a hazel croft,

And up aloft dim larks winged strong.

And I, too, told the kings a story

Of later glory, her fourth sorrow:

There was a sound like moving shields

In high green fields and the lowland furrow.

And one said : " We who yet are kings

Have heard these things lamenting inly."

Sweet music flowed from many a bill

And on the hill the morn stood queenly.

And one said : " Over is the singing,

And bell bough ringing, whence we come ;

With heavy hearts we'll tread the shadows,

In honey meadows birds are dumb."

And one said : " Since the poets perished

And all they cherished in the way,

D

Their thoughts unsung, like petal showers

Inflame the hours of blue and gray."

And one said : " A loud tramp of men

We'll hear again at Rosnaree."

A bomb burst near me where I lay.

I woke, 'twas day in Picardy.

France,
January 7th, 1917.

IN FRANCE

THE silence of maternal hills

Is round me in my evening dreams ;

And round me music-making bills

And mingling waves of pastoral streams.

Whatever way I turn I find

The path is old unto me still.

The hills of home are in my mind,

And there I wander as I will.

February 3rd, 1917.

HAD I A GOLDEN POUND
(AFTER THE IRISH)

HAD I a golden pound to spend,

My love should mend and sew no more.

And I would buy her a little quern,

Easy to turn on the kitchen floor.

And for her windows curtains white,

With birds in flight and flowers in bloom,

To face with pride the road to town,

And mellow down her sunlit room.

And with the silver change we'd prove

The truth of Love to life's own end,

With hearts the years could but embolden,

Had I a golden pound to spend.

February 5th, 1917.

FAIRIES

MAIDEN-POET, come with me
To the heaped up cairn of Maeve,
And there we'll dance a fairy dance
Upon a fairy's grave.

In and out among the trees,
Filling all the night with sound,
The morning, strung upon her star,
Shall chase us round and round.

What are we but fairies too,

Living but in dreams alone,

Or, at the most, but children still,

Innocent and overgrown ?

February 6th, 1917.

IN A CAFÉ

Kiss the maid and pass her round,
Lips like hers were made for many.
Our loves are far from us to-night,
But these red lips are sweet as any.

Let no empty glass be seen
Aloof from our good table's sparkle,
At the acme of our cheer
Here are francs to keep the circle.

They are far who miss us most—

Sip and kiss—how well we love them,

Battling through the world to keep

Their hearts at peace, their God above them.

February 11*th*, 1917.

SPRING

ONCE more the lark with song and speed

Cleaves through the dawn, his hurried bars

Fall, like the flute of Ganymede

Twirling and whistling from the stars.

The primrose and the daffodil

Surprise the valleys, and wild thyme

Is sweet on every little hill,

When lambs come down at folding time.

In every wild place now is heard

The magpie's noisy house, and through

The mingled tunes of many a bird
The ruffled wood-dove's gentle coo.

Sweet by the river's noisy brink
The water-lily bursts her crown,
The kingfisher comes down to drink
Like rainbow jewels falling down.

And when the blue and grey entwine
The daisy shuts her golden eye,
And peace wraps all those hills of mine
Safe in my dearest memory.

France,
  March 8th, 1917.

PAN

HE knows the safe ways and unsafe
And he will lead the lambs to fold,
Gathering them with his merry pipe,
The gentle and the overbold.

He counts them over one by one,
And leads them back by cliff and steep,
To grassy hills where dawn is wide,
And they may run and skip and leap.

PAN

And just because he loves the lambs

He settles them for rest at noon,

And plays them on his oaten pipe

The very wonder of a tune.

France,
  March 11th, 1917.

WITH FLOWERS

THESE have more language than my song,
Take them and let them speak for me.
I whispered them a secret thing
Down the green lanes of Allary.

You shall remember quiet ways
Watching them fade, and quiet eyes,
And two hearts given up to love,
A foolish and an overwise.

France,
April, 1917.

THE FIND

I TOOK a reed and blew a tune,
And sweet it was and very clear
To be about a little thing
That only few hold dear.

Three times the cuckoo named himself,
But nothing heard him on the hill,
Where I was piping like an elf
The air was very still.

'Twas all about a little thing

I made a mystery of sound,

I found it in a fairy ring

Upon a fairy mound.

June 2nd, 1917.

A FAIRY HUNT

Who would hear the fairy horn
Calling all the hounds of Finn
Must be in a lark's nest born
When the moon is very thin.

I who have the gift can hear
Hounds and horn and tally ho,
And the tongue of Bran as clear
As Christmas bells across the snow.

And beside my secret place
Hurries by the fairy fox,
With the moonrise on his face,
Up and down the mossy rocks.

Then the music of a horn
And the flash of scarlet men,
Thick as poppies in the corn
All across the dusky glen.

Oh ! the mad delight of chase !
Oh ! the shouting and the cheer !
Many an owl doth leave his place
In the dusty tree to hear.

TO ONE WHO COMES NOW
AND THEN

WHEN you come in, it seems a brighter fire
Crackles upon the hearth invitingly,
The household routine which was wont to
    tire
Grows full of novelty.

You sit upon our home-upholstered chair
And talk of matters wonderful and strange,
Of books, and travel, customs old which
    dare
The gods of Time and Change.

Till we with inner word our care refute

Laughing that this our bosoms yet assails,

While there are maidens dancing to a flute

In Andalusian vales.

And sometimes from my shelf of poems you
　　take

And secret meanings to our hearts disclose,

As when the winds of June the mid bush
　　shake

We see the hidden rose.

And when the shadows muster, and each tree

A moment flutters, full of shutting wings,

You take the fiddle and mysteriously

Wake wonders on the strings..

And in my garden, grey with misty flowers,

Low echoes fainter than a beetle's horn

Fill all the corners with it, like sweet showers

Of bells, in the owl's morn.

Come often, friend, with welcome and sur-
      prise

We'll greet you from the sea or from the
      town ;

Come when you like and from whatever
      skies

Above you smile or frown.

   Belgium,
    July 22nd, 1917.

THE SYLPH

I SAW you and I named a flower
That lights with blue a woodland space,
I named a bird of the red hour
And a hidden fairy place.

And then I saw you not, and knew
Dead leaves were whirling down the mist,
And something lost was crying through
An evening of amethyst.

HOME

A BURST of sudden wings at dawn,
Faint voices in a dreamy noon,
Evenings of mist and murmurings,
And nights with rainbows of the moon.

And through these things a wood-way dim,
And waters dim, and slow sheep seen
On uphill paths that wind away
Through summer sounds and harvest green.

This is a song a robin sang

This morning on a broken tree,

It was about the little fields

That call across the world to me.

Belgium,
  July, 1917.

THE LANAWN SHEE

POWDERED and perfumed the full bee
Winged heavily across the clover,
And where the hills were dim with dew,
Purple and blue the west leaned over.

A willow spray dipped in the stream,
Moving a gleam of silver ringing,
And by a finny creek a maid
Filled all the shade with softest singing.

Listening, my heart and soul at strife,
On the edge of life I seemed to hover,

For I knew my love had come at last,

That my joy was past and my gladness over.

I tiptoed gently up and stooped

Above her looped and shining tresses,

And asked her of her kin and name,

And why she came from fairy places.

She told me of a sunny coast

Beyond the most adventurous sailor,

Where she had spent a thousand years

Out of the fears that now assail her.

And there, she told me, honey drops

Out of the tops of ash and willow,

And in the mellow shadow Sleep

Doth sweetly keep her poppy pillow.

Nor Autumn with her brown line marks

The time of larks, the length of roses,

But song-time there is over never

Nor flower-time ever, ever closes.

And wildly through uncurling ferns

Fast water turns down valleys singing,

Filling with scented winds the dales,

Setting the bells of sleep a-ringing.

And when the thin moon lowly sinks,

Through cloudy chinks a silver glory

Lingers upon the left of night

Till dawn delights the meadows hoary.

And by the lakes the skies are white,

(Oh, the delight !) when swans are coming,

Among the flowers sweet joy-bells peal,

And quick bees wheel in drowsy humming.

The squirrel leaves her dusty house

And in the boughs makes fearless gambol,

And, falling down in fire-drops, red,

The fruit is shed from every bramble.

Then, gathered all about the trees

Glad galaxies of youth are dancing,

Treading the perfume of the flowers,

Filling the hours with mazy glancing.

And when the dance is done, the trees

Are left to Peace and the brown woodpecker,

And on the western slopes of sky

The day's blue eye begins to flicker.

But at the sighing of the leaves,

When all earth grieves for lights departed

An ancient and a sad desire

Steals in to tire the human-hearted.

No fairy aid can save them now

Nor turn their prow upon the ocean,

The hundred years that missed each heart

Above them start their wheels in motion.

And so our loves are lost, she sighed,

And far and wide we seek new treasure,

For who on Time or Timeless hills

Can live the ills of loveless leisure ?

(" Fairer than Usna's youngest son,

O, my poor one, what flower-bed holds you?

Or, wrecked upon the shores of home,

What wave of foam with white enfolds you ?

" You rode with kings on hills of green,

And lovely queens have served you banquet,

Sweet wine from berries bruised they brought

And shyly sought the lips which drank it.

" But in your dim grave of the sea

There shall not be a friend to love you.

And ever heedless of your loss

The earth ships cross the storms above you.

" And still the chase goes on, and still

The wine shall spill, and vacant places

Be given over to the new

As love untrue keeps changing faces.

" And I must wander with my song

Far from the young till Love returning,

Brings me the beautiful reward

Of some heart stirred by my long yearning.")

Friend, have you heard a bird lament

When sleet is sent for April weather ?

As beautiful she told her grief,

As down through leaf and flower I led her.

And friend, could I remain unstirred

Without a word for such a sorrow ?

Say, can the lark forget the cloud

When poppies shroud the seeded furrow ?

Like a poor widow whose late grief

Seeks for relief in lonely byeways,

The moon, companionless and dim,
Took her dull rim through starless highways.

I was too weak with dreams to feel
Enchantment steal with guilt upon me,
She slipped, a flower upon the wind,
And laughed to find how she had won me.

From hill to hill, from land to land,
Her lovely hand is beckoning for me,
I follow on through dangerous zones,
Cross dead men's bones and oceans stormy.

Some day I know she'll wait at last
And lock me fast in white embraces,
And down mysterious ways of love
We two shall move to fairy places.

Belgium,
July, 1917.

ImTheStory.com

Personalized Classic Books in many genre's

Unique gift for kids, partners, friends, colleagues

Customize:

- Character Names
- Upload your own front/back cover images (optional)
- Inscribe a personal message/dedication on the
  inside page (optional)

Customize many titles Including
- Alice in Wonderland
- Romeo and Juliet
- The Wizard of Oz
- A Christmas Carol
- Dracula
- Dr. Jekyll & Mr. Hyde
- And more...

Emily's Adventures in Wonderland

Ryan & Julia

Lightning Source UK Ltd.
Milton Keynes UK
UKOW07f0152280115

245257UK00007B/137/P